Robert Morrison

Robert Morrison

Translator in China

AMBASSADOR INTERNATIONAL

Greenville, South Carolina • Belfast, Northern Ireland

Robert Morrison:
Translator in China

First printing, 2004
Printed in the United States of America

Cover design & page layout by A & E Media — Paula Shepherd
Cover illustration by Portland Studios — Justin Gerard
Edited by Rebecca Hammond

ISBN 1 932307 26 5

Published by the Ambassador Group

Ambassador Emerald International
427 Wade Hampton Blvd.
Greenville, SC 29609
USA
www. emeraldhouse.com

and

Ambassador Publications Ltd.
Providence House
Ardenlee Street
Belfast BT6 8QJ
Northern Ireland
www. ambassador-productions.com

The colophon is a trademark of Ambassador

Contents

PROLOGUE

hey shall mount up with wings as eagles; they shall run and not be weary; they shall walk and not faint." This verse in Isaiah chapter 40 captures the essence of Robert Morrison, the first Protestant missionary to China; the pioneer who, through long years of discouragement, doggedly worked to do everything he could to spread the Gospel of Jesus Christ in that vast and pagan land. His is the story of a man who was resolved to do his duty, however hard and irksome it might be, and for that reason, rather than because he was the first Protestant missionary to the Chinese, his story should be told and remembered.

It was easy at first to strive eagerly for the right; it was much more difficult to walk day by day along a dull and weary road and not feel so faint with the effort that he could no longer go on. It was the long and weary walk that Robert Morrison was called upon to do—often lonely, often discouraged, often feeling that with all his striving he was accomplishing little. His triumph is that he kept on, and his work, although not the work he wanted so eagerly to accomplish, was the one thing needed to help other missionaries coming after him in their great and difficult task. What he accomplished is not forgotten, and the way in which he carried out his task must help all people to realize that, however dull and plodding their work appears to be, if they can do as he did and go on doggedly doing what they know is right, their efforts will not be in vain.

CHAPTER 1

The Boy

1782-1802

obert Morrison was born on January 5, 1782, either at the little village of Wingates or at Morpeth, ten miles northwest. Both places are in Northumberland and while some accounts give Wingates and some Morpeth as his birthplace, what is certain is that the first three years of his life were spent at Bullers Green, Morpeth, where his father, James Morrison, was an agricultural worker.

Robert's father was a Scot who had married a Northumbrian girl, Hannah Nicholson, and Robert was the youngest of a family of eight. When he was three the family left their cottage home in the country and went to Newcastle, where James Morrison, who was not really strong enough for the heavy work he had been doing, became a last and boot-tree maker.

Newcastle, which was Robert's home until he was nearly twenty-one, was not in the least like the busy city it is today. He lived in the eighteenth century. Railways and the industrial revolution were things hardly dreamed about. The population of Newcastle was only about thirty thousand and the old city walls were still standing. The Tyne was a shallow stream instead of a deep river, and Robert sometimes wandered along the quayside and along the riverbanks, with his friend George Stephenson, who years later became famous for inventing the steam engine.

As they grew older, they became interested in different things. George was clever with his hands; Robert was not. He was much more interested in his lessons. He was not brilliant, but extremely persevering, and he made the most of the teaching given him by his uncle, James Nicholson, a schoolmaster in the city. He had a very good memory and found learning by heart easy. His father was an elder of a Scottish church in Newcastle, and the minister, the Rev. John Hutton, was interested in Robert. He taught him many of the Psalms in the Scottish Version and Robert enjoyed these lessons, so much so that it is recorded that at the age of twelve

> he repeated one evening the whole of the hundred and nineteenth Psalm. To try him, Mr. Hutton did not go straight forward, but took different parts, forward and backward. He nevertheless accomplished his task without a single mistake.

Robert was a serious boy, with a good deal of the "dour" Scots nature. He had practically no sense of humor and lacked the fun-loving, mischievous spirit found in most young boys. When he was thirteen he went to North Shields to work for one of his uncles, who was a pattern-ring maker. He was not a success.

"Young Morrison is a handless chap and never can make a wise-like ring," remarked his uncle, and Robert evidently agreed. He did not enjoy his work and he wanted a change. He did something that seems entirely unlike him; he joined a company of strolling players with whom he traveled the country. It was the very last kind of life for which he was fitted; he was much too stolid and solemn and the influence of his home was too strong for him to enjoy the company of people who habitually drank and swore and had no liking for religion.

To the great relief of his parents, he returned home and went to work for his father. He was then nearly fifteen and it was during the next year that he experienced conversion. He had a very real sense of sin in his life and became certain that the only worthwhile way to live was to become a follower of the Lord Jesus Christ. He now wanted to put God first, and to please Him in everything.

He joined his father's church and became a member of a praying society, which met every Monday evening in his father's workshop. His life was very full. All day from about six in the morning until seven or eight in the evening he was working at the bench, and in the evenings and on Sundays he was concentrating on his Bible studies and trying to make his religion practical by visiting the sick.

It seemed as if his determination to be a real Christian made him keener and more alert in every way. It was at this time that he began to study with a view to educating himself, finding this not at all easy because he had not many books and only the vaguest idea of what things he ought to try to learn. He tried to learn botany, arithmetic and astronomy and found them uphill work. He had taught himself a system of shorthand in which he began to write a diary, which he continued, with only one short break, until he finally sailed for China. It showed very clearly how hard he was working. It showed, too, that he was by no means sure that he was wasting his time in reading things he found hard to understand. There is an entry in his diary for March 11, 1800, which reads: "I have adopted a number of studies—botany and some other things. I do not know but it would be better to study my Bible."

But his discouragement did not prevent him from going on trying to learn all he could. While he was working at last-making he would have a book propped up on his bench so that he could work and read at the same time, and he finally cleared up a space in a corner of the workshop and made up a bed for himself on the floor, so that he could study late at night and early in the morning undisturbed.

Years afterwards Robert, remembering this odd bedroom and study in the workshop, wrote:

> The happiest abode (so far as the house goes) was my father's workshop, swept clean by my own hands of a Saturday evening, and dedicated to prayer and mediation on the Sunday. There was my bed, and there was my study.

An entry in his diary about the time he began to study in earnest shows how tired he often was.

"After family worship I sat down to read a work upon astronomy but could not through weariness." No wonder, since he was stealing time from his much-needed sleep. This was probably the cause of the constant headaches he mentioned and to which he was subject all his life.

By the beginning of 1801 he had made up his mind that the work he really wanted to do was that of a minister. He knew that if he were to do this he must work harder than ever and learn things that up to now he had not attempted. The minister of one of the Presbyterian Churches in Newcastle was the Rev. Adam Laidlow. He was also a teacher, and Robert arranged to have lessons in Latin from him. The fee was a guinea as entrance money and a guinea a quarter afterwards. In order to earn the money, he had to work harder than ever at last-making, often working at the bench late at night to make up for the time spent with his tutor during the day.

He had at last found something that really interested him. There is no doubt that he had a real gift for languages, and during the next eighteen months he not only learned all the Latin he could but actually began Greek and Hebrew. And as he worked, his desire to become a minister of Christ and, if possible, a missionary to the heathen, grew greater, until at last his parents realized to what end he was working.

His mother was not only startled but also dismayed when she found out what her youngest and best-loved son wanted to do. She was not strong and she felt she could not bear to part with him. Robert, knowing that it would not be long before he was separated from her forever, promised not to leave home while she still lived. In 1802 she died and he felt he was now free to take the first real steps in what he knew would be his life work.

CHAPTER 2

The Young Man

1802-1805

obert Morrison was now twenty years of age, and on November 24, 1802, shortly after his mother's death, he wrote to the Hoxton Academy, which was a training college for Congregational ministers in London, asking to be received as a candidate for the ministry. He was accepted at once and, much against the wish of his father, he set sail from Newcastle to London.

It was not a comfortable voyage, and Morrison was a bad sailor. He was, however, happy to find among the passengers people of like mind to himself. In a letter to his father, he says:

I was happily surprised, when lying sick in the state room, by hearing a number of persons sing Psalms in the cabin; and every night when the weather would permit, we had prayers and reading of the Scriptures. The passage was very rough, in some parts of it; one night they let the ship drive, and another night pitched away her bowsprit, which last occurrence was very serious, as it endangered the loss of our masts.

I mention these circumstances to excite thankfulness to God, who brought us safely through. I pleaded the promise, in its literal sense, 'when thou passest through the waters I will be with thee,' and blessed be God, it was fulfilled.

This was the first rough sea passage Morrison had encountered but it was by no means his last. He was to experience many more during the course of his life.

He stayed for two years as a student at Hoxton. Never once did he doubt that he was following the right path. If he had done so, he would certainly have answered a letter he received from his father shortly after he had entered the college, in a very different manner.

His father wrote telling him that the business was suffering because of his absence, adding that he himself was not well, and asking his son to give up his project and return home. It must have been very painful to Robert to receive this letter, and answering it as he felt he must can only have been hard. He did not hesitate, however. He had no doubt that it was God Who had called him and that he must answer the call. Like the disciples of old, he knew he was called upon to forsake all and follow Him, and there could be no choice in the matter.

He wrote and told his father what he felt, in more than one letter. "Having set my hand to the plough, I would not turn back," he wrote. "I cannot help being much affected, so long as there is reason to suspect that you are offended with me. Your welfare in time and eternity is, and I hope ever shall be, near my heart."

His two years at Hoxton cannot have been altogether happy ones. As he studied and worked, preaching sometimes in the villages round London, letters came at intervals from Newcastle, and each letter urged him to return. Robert, although his nature was stern and dour, had a strong affection for his family and their lack of understanding hurt him greatly. It was now that his stubborn Scottish nature helped to strengthen him. Plead as they might, he would not yield. And all the time his thoughts were turning more and more towards the Mission Field. In his diary, he asked for guidance.

"Jesus," he wrote,

I have given myself up to Thy service. The question with me is where shall I serve Thee? I learn from Thy Word that it is Thy holy pleasure that the Gospel shall be preached in all the world. My desire, is, O Lord, to engage where laborers are most wanted. Perhaps one part of the field is more difficult than another. I am equally unfit for any, but through Thy strengthening me, I can do all things. O Lord, guide me in this. Enable me to count the cost, and having come to a resolution, to act consistently.

It was no light decision he had to make. He knew that his father would be strongly opposed to him becoming a missionary. His tutor at Hoxton was also against the idea, and advised him to be content with using his gifts at home. Robert listened to the advice, prayed about it, and was surer than ever that his duty was to become a missionary, and on May 27, 1804, he wrote to the London Missionary Society asking them to accept him.

The committee called him to an interview, and he replied to the questions they asked him so satisfactorily that he was at once accepted. His reply to an unusual question put to him by the chairman, shows very strongly his Scottish caution.

"Do you look upon the heathen as the angels do?" said the chairman.

Robert hesitated, then answered. "I don't know how the angels regard them, so I can't say 'Yes,' can I?" It was a sensible and shrewd answer for so young a man to make.

He was sent to the Missionary Academy at Gosport, and settled down to work there with his usual dogged determination. One of his fellow students said years later:

He was a remarkable man while at college, studious beyond most others, grave almost to gloom, abstracted, somewhat morose, but evidently absorbed in the contemplation of the great object which seemed to be ever swelling into more awful magnitude and grandeur the nearer he approached it.

Robert was thoroughly enjoying his studies. Latin he already knew fairly well, but Greek was another matter. He found at once that his friends were much further advanced in this subject and he had not the least intention of allowing this to continue. With his usual dogged determination he worked literally night and day, with the result that in an incredibly short time he had caught them up and was able to continue easily with the rest of his classmates.

In other things he was not quite so happy. His family were still thoroughly disapproving of his decision to become a missionary and their letters to him were not nearly so frequent as the young man, lonely for his home and people, wanted. His home letters show this very clearly. On one occasion he wrote to his brother:

I hope you will fulfill the promise you made in C's letter, to write to me soon. I must say that I have considered the silence of my friends and relatives as a very great unkindness: it has given me considerable uneasiness at different times. I hoped that you and my father would have written oftener.

Poor Robert! Most of his life his path was a lonely and hard one, which could have been made much less hard if the people he loved had kept in closer touch with him.

He was, of course, uncertain where he would be sent when his training was finished. His own inclination was towards Africa. Something was happening, however, which made the authorities decide to send him to an entirely different field of work.

For six years previously Dr. W. Moseley, of Hanley, had been trying to form a society for translating the Bible into Chinese. He had approached bishops, clergy and ministers of all sections of the Christian Church. Until the time when Robert Morrison was studying at Gosport he did not meet with any success. Everyone was interested and sure that the idea was a good and necessary one, but they did not see how it could be done. They felt the cost would be far more than could be met, and that even if this could be overcome, it would be impossible to get the books into China, except through the Roman Catholic missionaries, the only missionaries who were allowed by the Chinese to work there.

One of the people most interested in the idea was Dr. Bogue, the Principal of the Training College at Gosport, and it may have been he who finally managed to influence the Directors of the London Missionary Society to decide at last to seek for a suitable man to proceed to China with the object of learning the language and then translating the Scriptures into Chinese. They were sure that no man could learn sufficient Chinese in England to do this, and they were also sure that ordinary missionary work would not be possible in China at that time.

Dr. Bogue, thoughtfully considering whether any of the students under his charge were fitted for this very difficult task, knew at once that very few of them would be suitable. When he looked at Robert Morrison, however, it was different. Here was a man with exactly the characteristics needed: dogged, quiet determination, intense faith in and reliance upon God, fervent zeal for the spread of Christ's Kingdom, and added to these a gift for learning languages and a real love for study and hard work.

Dr. Bogue recommended him to the London Missionary Society and the recommendation was accepted. Robert was told what he was to do and, in spite of his desire to go to Africa, raised no objection. He had prayed to be given a hard and difficult task and his prayer had certainly been granted.

CHAPTER 3

Preparation for the Great Adventure

1805-1807

or more than two thousand years, China had shut itself away from the rest of the world. The Great Wall had been a complete defense on three sides and the seacoast was guarded from intruders. A few Roman Catholic missionaries had managed to penetrate into this guarded land and the Portuguese had gained an uncertain footing. For certain months of the year the East India Company was permitted to trade at Canton, but with great restrictions. China—haughty, self-sufficient, regarded herself as superior to the rest of the world and had not the slightest wish to allow the "barbarians," as she termed the people of the West, to penetrate her shores. And now it was to be left to one man to try to open the door to the Protestant missionaries and to bring the faith in which they believed to the surging masses of this haughty race. It seemed an almost impossible task.

It had not been intended at first that Robert Morrison should set out alone. The original idea of the Society was to send three or four men, but it proved impossible to obtain them. Years later Morrison remarked that the failure to send more than one man was a very good thing. It was difficult enough for him to obtain a footing when he first went; if more had gone they would have been forced to leave at once.

In August 1805 he was told that he must go either to London or Edinburgh for further studies. He went to London, walking each day from Bishopgate where he lodged to the Greenwich Observatory to study astronomy, and attending lectures at St. Bartholomew's Hospital to study medicine, knowing well that both these subjects would be useful for his future work. To begin to learn Chinese was more difficult, but here, unexpectedly, the way opened for him.

Dr. Mosely was walking one day down Leadenhall Street when he saw coming towards him a well-dressed Chinese gentleman. A few days later he sent for Morrison and told him of this meeting.

"I could not let him pass," he said, "because my heart was full of China. I spoke to him and asked him to come and dine with me. He did so, and during the evening he told me that a young Chinese of good education, named Yong Sam-tuk, had just come from Canton to study English and was living in Clapham. Come with me and see him. I think perhaps he might consent to teach you Chinese."

They went to see Yong Sam-tuk, who was willing to fall in with the plan. He came to share Morrison's lodgings and they began their work.

It was not easy for either of them. The customs of the East and West were very different. Morrison soon found out that his young Chinese friend was proud and domineering and that he had a fierce temper. Morrison often offended him without in the least meaning to do so.

Sam-tuk began to teach him the Chinese characters, which are used instead of letters. He employed the method used to teach boys in China to write. It was interesting but difficult to the Englishman. The characters to be learned were covered with a sheet of thin, transparent paper. Then Morrison was given a small stiff brush and told to trace over and over every line of the characters, holding the brush absolutely upright between the second and third fingers, until he was so familiar with the outlines of the characters that he knew them off by heart. It was a very tiring process, and it led to an outburst of fury from Yong Sam-tuk that was quite unexpected by Morrison.

He had been working for some time tracing the characters, until he was sure he knew them. Without thinking, he crumpled the paper and threw it in the fire before taking another sheet. To his amazement, Sam-tuk stormed at him, furiously indignant. Then he stalked out of the room, saying he would not give Morrison any more lessons. His indignation lasted for three days, during which he kept to his resolve. It was not until Robert understood that to the Chinese any paper with Chinese characters upon it is considered sacred and that burning it must be done with great ceremony, and had apologized very humbly for the offence he had given, that he could persuade the young Chinese to continue the lessons.

To prevent any possibility of such a thing happening again, Robert found a large tin plate and inscribed the characters on that instead of on paper. He felt it was safer to use something that he could not thoughtlessly throw into the fire!

Writing to his father about his work he remarked: "If I take the Chinese I am now with as a specimen of their disposition, it is a very bad one. He is obstinate, jealous and averse to speaking of things of God. He says 'my country –not custom to talky of God's business.'" Definitely Robert found it difficult to understand the ideas of his Chinese friend.

A Chinese manuscript had just been found among some documents in the British Museum, but no one had yet been able to decipher it. Yong Sam-tuk and Morrison were sure that between them they could do this, so for the next few months they visited the Museum daily. After some work they discovered that the manuscript was a Harmony of the Gospels, the Book of Acts and all Paul's Epistles. With it was also the manuscript of a Latin-Chinese dictionary. As far as they could discover the whole thing was the work of a Catholic missionary in China in the sixteenth century. Translating this manuscript was very good practice for Morrison and proved more useful than his lessons in speaking Chinese, although at the time he did not realize this.

The time was drawing near for his departure. In the late summer of 1806 he went back to Newcastle to say good-bye to his relatives there. The time he spent with them was filled with mixed emotions—happiness to be with them once more and sadness because he knew very well that he was going into unknown dangers and might never see them again.

It was not very easy to arrange a passage to the Far East. The East India Company, which had the monopoly of trade in India and the East, had always refused to allow missionaries to travel on their ships. The usual custom was for missionaries to travel on ships of other nations, and although the Directors of the London Missionary Society tried to get the East India Company to make an exception in Morrison's case, they refused to agree, and it was finally arranged that he should sail first to America and proceed to Canton from there.

It was on January 7, 1807, that, together with two missionaries who were going to India, Morrison was ordained to the work of the ministry in the Scots Church, Swallow Street.

"A day never to be forgotten," wrote Morrison in his diary. "I was this evening solemnly ordained to the ministry of the Gospel among the heathen. Oh, that the engagements of this evening may be sanctioned in Heaven!"

In the letter of instructions that he received from the Society before he sailed, he was given full liberty to act "on every occasion according to the dictates of your own prudence and discretion," a very necessary instruction considering that he would be entirely alone in his work. The Society knew that it was very unlikely that he would be able to do the ordinary work of a missionary in China. All they hoped was that he would be able to stay in Canton long enough to learn the language, compile a Chinese Dictionary and translate the Bible, and they knew that this task would certainly take him a good many years to complete.

CHAPTER 4

On the Way

January, 1807-September, 1807

orrison sailed in the *Remittance*, and in a letter to his father he confessed that, as they sailed down to Gravesend, he broke down and "wept bitterly." He was completely alone, he might never see his loved ones again, and for a short time he felt that the task he had undertaken was beyond him. But his trust in God was too great to allow these feelings to continue. He prayed: "O God, my Savior, go with me!" and his prayer was answered.

The journey was a very trying one. Today the voyage is not difficult; in those days, with only sailing ships completely dependent on the winds and tides, it was very different. For six weeks the *Remittance* lay in the Downs off Deal, waiting for a favorable wind. Then came a terrific storm. Many of the other ships waiting also, were driven ashore and some were sunk, while the anchor of the *Remittance* snapped and the mizzen and foresails split into shreds. Under bare poles the ship scudded down the Channel, with seas running mountains high and through a snowstorm so thick that the crew could not see as far as the length of the ship.

> In the midst of our extremity," wrote Morrison, "an alarm was raised that the ship was on fire, owing to the bursting of some bottles of vitriol. The pilot and one of the men leaped into the mizzen chains in order to jump overboard, preferring death by drowning than to be burned alive. Happily, however, the other men had courage enough to seize the bottles and push them overboard.

At last the gale died down, fresh sails were run up, and the ship went on her way. It was February 28th when they were finally out of sight of land. As Morrison stood watching the last glimpse of the Isle of Wight fading into the distance, tears ran down his cheeks. He knew that it might be the last time he saw the land that he loved so well.

As the voyage went on he tried to study but found this almost impossible because of the gales. "I stood on deck," he wrote in his diary on March 29th, "until I was completely drenched, helping to take in the last rag of sail and to pump the ship." And two days later he wrote: "It is now judged prudent to put us on an allowance of water. Our fresh provisions begin to fail. All of us are much indisposed."

The storm continued for eleven days, the ship drifting to the southeast. "For the past twenty-five days," he wrote, "we have not advanced one step towards our desired haven."

On the following Saturday evening, they sighted a brig flying signals of distress. The *Remittance* bore round to find out what was wrong, but could not get within speaking distance before dusk. Then they learned that the vessel was almost waterlogged and could not carry sail without opening her planks. For eleven days and nights her crew had been working desperately at the pumps. All the *Remittance* could do that night was to stand by and wait until morning. The greater part of the next day was spent in saving the crew of eleven men and as much of the provisions from the ship as possible. As soon as this was done the brig was set on fire, so that she could not continue drifting to the danger of other vessels.

On April 20th, after having been about one hundred days at sea, the *Remittance* cast anchor off New York. Here for the next three weeks the missionaries received great kindness and hospitality, and Morrison in particular was given invaluable help, without which he would certainly not have been able to proceed.

Dr. Green, of Philadelphia, where Morrison stayed for two days, at once promised to give all the help he could and a letter was sent to Washington to ask for a letter of introduction for Morrison to the American

Consul at Canton. The Secretary of State generously agreed to this, and a berth on the American ship *Trident,* bound for Canton, was secured for him on payment only of his board, a very generous concession.

It is interesting to record the impression made by Morrison on the American who acted as his host. He wrote,

> He was civil rather than affable, with a temperament naturally firm and somewhat haughty; solemn but pleasant; plain, simple and unceremonious. His was evidently a rugged nature, not given to display of sentiment. His piety had the bark on.

There was another side to his nature, however, and that was his liking for children. His host wrote, "As the notice of his arrival had been short, he was placed for the first night in our own bedroom. By the side of his bed stood a crib in which slept my little child. On waking in the morning she turned as usual to talk to her mother. Seeing a stranger where she expected to have found her parents, she roused herself with a look of alarm, then, fixing her eyes steadily upon his face she asked, 'Man, do you pray to God?' 'Oh yes, my dear,' said Mr. Morrison, 'every day. God is my best friend.' At once reassured, the little girl laid her head contentedly on her pillow and fell fast asleep." And for the rest of Morrison's stay they were the best of friends.

On the day on which he was due to sail he had to go to the counting house of the owner of the *Trident.* The merchant, as he handed his papers to Morrison, looked at him with an amused smile, obviously thinking he was a deluded enthusiast. Then he said with a grin, "And so, Mr. Morrison, you really expect that you will make an impression on the idolatry of the great Chinese Empire?"

"No, sir," said Morrison with more than his usual sternness. "I expect God will!" and with this fitting retort he turned and stalked out of the office.

On May 12, the *Trident* sailed from New York. The journey took them round Cape Horn and across the Pacific, and they were at sea one hundred and nineteen days. Again it was a difficult voyage. As before mentioned, Morrison was not a good sailor, and within a few hours he records that he was "fully as sick as ever I was, for at least a week."

As the weather grew warmer the temperature in his cabin was like an oven, and he was glad to be allowed to use the roundhouse on deck for his study, with its many windows wide open to catch the breeze. Here he worked hard at Chinese, Hebrew and Greek, finding it almost impossible to take necessary exercise on deck because the deck itself was so hot and the sun so fierce that walking outside the roundhouse made him feel ill.

On June 17th, they "crossed the line," and the usual horse-play was indulged in by the sailors: the new hands and even some of the passengers were shaved with tar and hoop-iron and dunked many times in a barrel of sea-water by order of Neptune and Aphrodite. Fortunately for Morrison, the captain refused to allow the sailors to treat him in this manner. If they had done so, he would probably have found it very difficult to keep his temper— he was far too solemn to enjoy such rough jokes!

As the voyage went on, the *Trident* had to face ugly seas. On one occasion a wave as high as the mizzen topsail drove the ship broadside to the wind, where she lay for some time in great peril nearly on her beam-ends, while the weight of water forced open the doors of the roundhouse, where Morrison was trying to work, and washed him from his seat.

It was not until Sunday, September 7th, nearly nine months after he left Gravesend, that the neighborhood of Canton was safely reached, and the young missionary— he was now twenty-five years of age—had his first glimpse of the strange land he had so longed to reach. He stood watching as the ship dropped anchor in the Macao Roads, and his heart beat fast with the thought that now at last his great adventure was really about to begin.

CHAPTER 5

Canton

1807-1808

lthough the headquarters of the East India Company were at Canton, they were not in the city itself. All foreigners were obliged to live on a plot of ground on the north bank of the Pearl River, outside the city walls. This plot had a river frontage of about one thousand feet from east to west, while the average depth was about seven hundred feet, giving three hundred feet of open space in front, facing the river. The buildings of the various trading companies, American, French, Spanish, Dutch, as well as English, formed a solid block intersected by two or three narrow streets and were known as the Factories, because the Factors lived there.

Each Factory was divided into three or more houses and was built of brick or granite, two stories high, standing up oddly amongst the squat, one-storied Chinese dwellings. The ground on which they stood was actually a mud flat and was liable to be flooded at high water. No women were allowed to live there, and the merchants' families were obliged to live at Macao, an island belonging partly to the Portuguese, at the mouth of the Pearl River opposite Canton. The trading season was six months in each year, during which time the merchants and their families were separated, the merchants returning to Macao for the remaining six months when the trading fleet was absent.

The *Trident* had anchored in the Macao Roads, so Morrison went ashore at Macao, and there he had the unexpected pleasure of meeting Sir George Staunton, Interpreter to the East India Company, whom he had already met in London, and Mr. Chalmers, to whom he had a letter of introduction.

Neither of these officials was encouraging as to Morrison's prospect of success in his work.

Mr. Chalmers, the chief of the East India Company's Factory at Macao, said gloomily:

> I wish you success with all my soul, but I must tell you that the people of Europe have no idea of the difficulty of living here or of obtaining native teachers. The Chinese are forbidden to teach the language to foreigners on penalty of death.

"Yes, that is quite correct," remarked Sir George. "Besides that, I must remind you that the Company forbids any person to stay at Canton except to trade. Personally I will do all in my power to help you, but I am afraid you will not be able to live at Canton, and to live here at Macao will be difficult, owing to the jealousy of the Roman Catholic Bishop and priests."

In spite of these gloomy remarks, Morrison was determined to try to live at Canton. He went to see Mr. Carrington, chief of the American Factory, to whom he had letters of introduction. Mr. Carrington offered to allow him to stay in his house, but discussing this with Mr. Milner, another American, they decided that it would be less public if he stayed with Mr. Milner, who was not quite so important a person. It would also be cheaper and that was something to be considered.

Morrison knew that it was quite probable that the East India Company might object to him, an Englishman, living with Americans, but nothing could be decided about this until Mr. Chalmers and Sir George arrived at Canton, which would be at the beginning of the trading season in about a month or six weeks time. In the meantime he settled down to wait for them, beginning his studies at once by himself.

He was appalled by the expense of living at Canton. Most of his letters home at this time are full of this, mentioning the cost of rent and board and even the price of candles and laundry. His rooms in Mr. Milner's house were entirely his own, and he was forced, so that he could continue his own work, to employ three Chinese servants, a boy to run errands and make his bed, a coo-lee, (as he spells the word coolie) to bring water and do rough work, and a cook. While living there he managed to buy various Chinese books, writing home to say that he had obtained about five hundred volumes on language, religion, philosophy, medicine, and a code of laws and history. A little later these books had risen in number to one thousand two hundred and twenty-nine! Morrison knew that the Chinese who had procured them for him had considerably overcharged him, but he knew this could not be helped.

When Sir George finally arrived, he managed to engage two Chinese teachers for Morrison: one was Abel Yun, a young Roman Catholic, who could speak Latin fluently but could not read his own language, although he could teach Morrison to speak Mandarin, the official Chinese language; the other was Le Seen Sing, an educated native who could write and had a degree as a man of letters, and who could teach Morrison to speak Cantonese.

Just as Morrison had to pay more than the usual price for Chinese books, so now the same thing happened with the salaries of his Chinese teachers. He had been told that ten dollars a month was what he should pay, but on giving

Abel this he saw at once that the man was not satisfied. After the next lesson Abel put a paper in his hands asking thirty dollars a month, and Morrison, knowing that if he did not get this amount Abel would certainly stop teaching him, was obliged to pay it.

All this time he was living almost in hiding, hardly ever going out, and he now found that his health was suffering from lack of fresh air and exercise. Finally he ventured out into the suburbs where foreigners were permitted to go but were not welcomed. He records that the streets were narrow lanes with an open drain down the middle. Everywhere was crowded. The shops were small but loaded with stock and open to the street. The shopkeeper often spread his goods on the pavement, so that when customers were buying there was scarcely room for people to pass.

Walking was difficult and made more unpleasant by the amount of notice he, as a foreigner, attracted.

"The Chinese followed me," he wrote, "calling me names, and crowding round the shop at which I stopped, as children in Newcastle do when a Turk or other foreigner passes along. The laboring Chinese here wear very little clothing; neither hat nor anything like shirt, or waistcoat, or jacket or shoes or stockings."

It was not long before the Chinese, who are very quick-witted, realized that this foreigner was different from most of the others. Some said he was a rich man, or at least the son of one, because in no other way could they account for his presence in Canton, or for the fact that he did not want to "make good profits." Others came much too near the truth and said he was an American missionary.

"This, I perceive, is not grateful to some of the Americans!" wrote Morrison.

Before long Morrison realized that to learn to speak and write Chinese was considerably more difficult than he had thought in England. The spoken tongue varied considerably. There could be one word for an object when written and two or three when spoken. He knew that it would certainly be a long time before he could begin the work he wished to do: the translation of the Scriptures.

He was very interested in the religious rites and customs of the Chinese, and they filled him with disgust and amazement. He could not understand how such an intellectual people could be idol worshippers. To honor their gods they lit lanterns, held theatrical performances and places stacks of food in front of the idols, and he could not see how this kind of thing had anything to do with religion.

He visited a temple to a god called Poo-sa, and found it filled with worshippers and thick with smoke from the altars. Fragrant matches and gilt paper were lit and thrown on the metal altar, while a priest beat a large drum and clanged a bell.

"There is nothing social in their worship nor any respect shown to each other," he wrote. "While one is praying, another is talking and laughing and a third cleaning utensils; while Poo-sa is smoked, smutted and almost burnt out of his dwelling."

Living where he did was proving very expensive, so Morrison moved to two empty rooms in the old French Factory building, now vacant. He thought it would probably be more economical to live as a Chinese and that by dressing as they did he would attract less attention when he went out.

He carried out this idea. He ate like a Chinese, using chopsticks and eating Chinese food, mostly rice. He wore a Chinese frock and thick Chinese shoes. He allowed his nails to grow long as the Chinese did and even wore a long tress of hair as a pigtail. He ate with his native teachers, and worked by the light of an earthenware lamp, screened from the draught by propping up a large folio volume of Matthew Henry's Commentary standing open on its edge, a purpose for which it had certainly not been intended!

This mode of life was a big mistake. The Chinese food did not suit him. When he went out the Chinese, so far from not noticing him, followed him about more than ever. He was a foreigner! Why, then, did he not dress as one? Was he a spy? Certainly he must be dangerous!

Morrison, finding out what was happening, was sensible enough to go back to his own manners and customs. His teachers were by now becoming almost fond of him. He was of exactly the right nature to win their approval. His grave and solemn manner seemed to them very dignified, and his lack of humor did not worry them. Mr. Yong, the young Chinese student who had helped in London, now came to his help again, using all his good influence with one of the leading Chinese security merchants named Gow-Qua to allow Morrison to remain in Canton.

By the time Morrison had been eight months in Canton his health was beginning to seriously to break down. He was working far too hard at his studies and taking insufficient exercise. More than once as the days went on he was forced to stop work and go early to bed, and on some days was so ill that he could not work at all.

His friends, seeing this, began to be seriously alarmed. They implored him to give in to his ill health for a time and to go to Macao for a rest. Reluctantly he agreed, but even then, so little did he want to have his work interrupted, he put off his departure from day to day on one excuse after another. At last, he felt so ill that he realized that they were right and he was wrong. On the last day of May he set sail for Macao in a Chinese junk. He was broken in health and for the time being beaten, but as determined as ever to resume his labors as soon as he could.

CHAPTER 6

The Way Made Plain

1808-1812

obert Morrison stayed for three months in Macao. Mr. Roberts, Chief of the Canton English Factory, offered to allow him to stay at his house and this was a good thing, because otherwise he would not have been permitted to remain. The Roman Catholics were all-powerful in Macao and they naturally resented the intrusion of a Protestant missionary on what they considered their own ground.

As he was under Mr. Roberts' protection, however, they could not interfere with him, and he lived quietly there, continuing his studies—his Chinese teachers had accompanied him—and planning out his ambitious project, the compilation of an English-Chinese Dictionary. Mr. Roberts and another of the English colony were very interested in this, so much so that they offered practical help. This was the offer of two houses, in Macao and in Canton, where he would be able to live quietly without much fear of interference.

By this time Morrison's knowledge of Chinese had increased greatly, and he had already done a little work on the Dictionary. By the time he returned to Canton with his health greatly improved, work on this was part of his regular daily routine. This quiet life was, however, again interrupted.

Two months after he returned to Canton, a violent dispute arose between the English and Chinese Governments. The English were at war with France and it was feared that the French might try to seize Macao. Lord Minto, Governor-General of India, sent a powerful squadron of ships and an armed force to land and hold Macao, and the Chinese, alarmed and furious, instantly took steps against the English.

They withdrew the right of trading at Canton and the Emperor sent a letter to this effect, which was a wonderful example of haughty superiority.

Knowing as you ought to know," it said, "that the Portuguese inhabit a territory belonging to the Celestial Empire, how could you suppose that the French would ever venture to molest them? If they dared, our warlike tribes would attack, defeat and chase them from the face of the country. Conscious of this truth, why did you bring your soldiers hither? Repent and withdraw immediately. The permission to trade shall then be restored; but should you persist in remaining, the hatches of your ships shall not be unlocked.

The Chinese Government then ordered the withdrawal of all Chinese servants from the Factories and stopped all supplies, so that the English were obliged to take refuge on ships in the harbor. Morrison had to leave Canton at a moment's notice, leaving his books behind in the care of his friend, Yong Sam-tuk.

One of his Chinese teachers, Low-Heen, went with him to Macao, but he went in daily fear of discovery and punishment, and before long Morrison was left alone. He records in his diary: "Teacher, assistants and servants left me today." It was a time of great trial and loneliness, made worse because of the non-arrival of letters from home. He had written dozens of letters and journals and sent them home, but few letters came to him. Four months after his arrival in China he wrote:

Permit me to say that I am considerably disappointed in not receiving from any person in England—from any of the brethren or fathers—letters by the fleet which sailed three months after I left my native land. I know how much all the ministers are engaged and also mercantile brethren, but it is by no means an object of no importance to write frequently and largely to missionaries among the heathen.

Eight months later, writing to a friend, he said:

I yesterday received your very welcome letter. It is but the second that I have received, after having written at least two hundred.

A few weeks later he remarked again:

Some of the good people who write to me grieve me by their manner. They say 'Write us long letters and tell us everything, but we are so full of business' or 'the ship is just going. Excuse our not giving you news.' As if they thought a missionary were an idle fellow who might take time whenever he chose to write them long letters, while I must be satisfied with a few apologies from them!

The house in which Morrison lived and worked in Macao was so dilapidated that the roof fell in and he and his helpers narrowly escaped injury. The landlord refused to repair the roof and then raised the rent, saying that Morrison was turning the house into a chapel—this because on Sundays the missionary read and prayed with his assistants when he could get them to listen. Morrison hardly dared to go out in daylight because of the feelings of the Roman Catholics towards him, and his exercise was done walking in the fields by moonlight, escorted by two of his Chinese friends.

He began to think that he had better leave Macao and go to Penang, where he was sure he could work undisturbed. It was when he had almost decided to do this that two things happened that changed his mind. The first was the acquisition of new friends. He met an Englishman, Dr. Morton, and his family. William Morton, the son, wanted to learn Chinese and began to come daily for this purpose. Morrison was, however, more interested in the daughter, Mary, and day by day he became more so. His journal at this time is interesting and rather amusing. It is evident that he was not sure that his love for her was not making him less diligent in his work.

"I spent the evening with Mr. Morton and family," he wrote. "By not applying to my studies my mind is uncomfortable." Two days later he wrote again. "I spent the evening with the family of the Mortons. Scarcely so devoted as I ought to be." Whether this referred to Mary or his studies he does not make clear, but it is obvious that his conscience was uneasy.

He was too much in love, however, to do anything but propose to her. Their marriage followed soon after. The Mortons were returning to England and before they left, on February 20, 1809, he and Mary were married. He had now determined definitely to go to Penang, but on his wedding day he had a most unexpected offer.

It came from the East India Company; the offer of a post as Chinese Translator to the English Factory at a salary of five hundred pounds a year, the exact sum he had spent during his first year in China.

This was a very great compliment. It proved that Sir George Staunton and the Factory Chiefs had been very much impressed with his mastery of the Chinese language. Morrison weighed the offer very carefully and had no hesitation in accepting it, making it clear at the same time that he must leave it to the London Missionary Society to confirm his appointment.

He wrote to them about it, stating his reasons for accepting it: first and most important, this official status would make his position at Canton safe, because as a member of the Company he had a right to be there; secondly, the duties would help him considerably with the language, because he would meet and talk to Chinese merchants and Government officials; thirdly, the salary would mean he would be less of an expense to the Missionary Society, and lastly, he was sure that his readiness to serve the Company ought to help them to be more tolerant of missionaries generally. Needless to say, the Missionary Society at once confirmed his appointment.

His domestic life began almost at once to be full of anxieties. His appointment meant that he would have

to be absent from Macao for about six months every year and, of course, his wife was not allowed by the Chinese to go with him to Canton. She was not strong and the separation, so soon after her marriage, resulted in a breakdown from which she never really recovered. It was arranged that she should stay with a Dr. Livingstone while Morrison was away, but although he looked after her, he had to tell her husband that her bad health was incurable. Later, keen sorrow was added to Morrison's anxiety; their first-born son died on the day of his birth, and in the midst of his sorrow, because the English had no cemetery at Macao, he had to obtain permission from the Chinese for some place where his son could be buried. It was only after great difficulty that he finally obtained permission for this to be on a spot on one of the hills to the north of the settlement.

His work was hard and exacting, and it did not give him nearly as much time as he wanted for the compilation of his dictionary and translations of the Bible. He knew that some people at home thought he had deserted his post and that hurt him bitterly. He himself was sometimes not certain that he had done the right thing in accepting his official post.

It occupies a great part of my short life in that which does not immediately refer to my first object," he wrote. "While I am translating official papers I could be compiling my dictionary.

My duties have given me many an aching head. The Chinese
Government dislikes hearing what I am obliged to tell them.
To be faithful and yet not impede myself in my missionary
work is a difficult thing. For the cause I serve, I would gladly
exchange my present situation for any in England and
Scotland of fifty pounds a year.

The salary he received he thought nothing of, except
that it would help him in his real work. When, later
on, Sir George Staunton left China and Morrison's
duties therefore increased, this was raised to £1,000 a
year, together with other privileges, but he would have
resigned his post immediately if by doing so he could
have devoted himself entirely to missionary work.

"My missionary duties require my whole undivided
time; every other pursuit is contrary to my feelings,"
he wrote, and he found it so difficult to do his official
work and his missionary work that at one time he
seriously thought of giving up his post and leaving for
Penang or Malacca.

I am at present much depressed on account of the trouble
occasioned by the Government here," he wrote. "It is my
heart's wish to go away to a more comfortable residence, where
freedom may be given to communicate fully and publicly the
Good Tidings. I have a strong impression in my mind that Java
would be a better place for our Mission. Direct us, O Lord, and
help us to put our trust in Thee.

In spite of these occasional doubts he really knew that God had called him to his present post and that to leave it would be desertion. He did his official work to the best of his powers and quietly continued with his dictionary and Bible translation, working late into the night. Sundays he kept for rest and worship, talking to his native helpers on religious subjects and reading the Bible with them. He did not seem to make much impression on them but he went quietly and steadily on, sure that if God willed, in time there would be the result he wished.

The amount of work he managed to do was amazing. By September 1812 he had sent to England three copies of the Acts of the Apostles in Chinese, a thousand copies of which had been printed in Macao by a Chinese printer. It had cost him $521, which he knew was a very high price. As the printer had run considerable risk in daring to print a foreigner's books, Morrison could not protest. He was able to arrange, however, that the wooden blocks from which the books had been printed should belong to him, so that later on he could print more copies. He had also sent a translation of St. Luke's Gospel and a Chinese Catechism and some tracts, and was beginning to translate the Book of Genesis.

Work on his Dictionary was still going on, and while he was working at his translations he had completed a Chinese Grammar, which Sir George Staunton considered extremely valuable, so much so that it was sent to Lord Minto, Governor-General of India, with the request that it should be printed there by the Government. Three years later, after considerable delay in a Government office at Calcutta, it was published.

In August 1812 a great joy came to Robert and Mary Morrison. Another baby was born to them, this time a girl, and the child lived and seemed strong and healthy. In December Morrison wrote to a friend:

> I am happy to say that Mrs. Morrison's health has considerably improved. She is deeply interested in the care of a little girl, now about five months old. Our dear babe enjoys good health. I have been from home about ten weeks. We have, however, the pleasure of hearing almost every day from each other.

Something else had happened that had brought great joy to Morrison. From time to time he had written to the London Missionary Society asking that another missionary should be sent out to help in the work of translation, and now at last he received the news that his request had been granted. William Milne, a young student of Gosport, two or three years younger than Morrison, was to come out to join him.

On September 4, 1812, Milne sailed from Portsmouth with his wife Rachel. She was a woman full of natural vivacity, which seemed "like the radiance of her eyes, unquenchable." She was exactly the right person to be a companion to Mary Morrison when their husbands were away from them. Small wonder that both the Morrisons looked forward to the arrival of the Milnes with eagerness and gladness.

Engraved by Jenkins, from a Painting by Chinnery in the Possession of Mrs Morrison

Yours faithfully
Robert Morrison

MORRISON WORKING WITH HIS CHINESE HELPERS

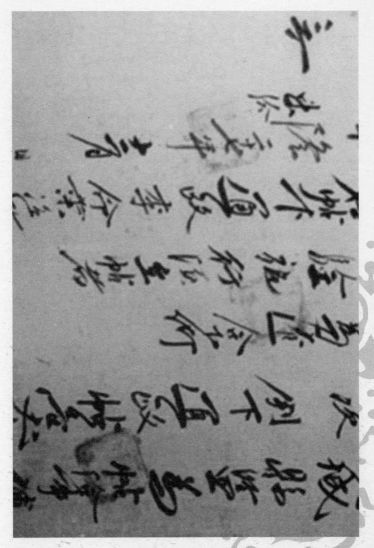

CHINESE CHARACTERS

GREAT WALL OF CHINA

LOCATION OF CHINA

ILLUSTRATION OF MORRISON IN CHINA

PORTRAIT OF MORRISON

CHAPTER 7

Difficulties and the First Convert

1812-1815

efore Mr. and Mrs. Milne arrived, something happened that made Morrison very worried for fear they would not be allowed to remain. For over a hundred years a law had been in force in Macao that forbade foreigners landing on the island to remain there. For a long time no one had paid any attention to it; now, suddenly, the Chinese decided to enforce it.

Morrison, who had taken a new house in Macao, decided that in the circumstances he had better take another smaller house next to his own, thinking that this might do for the Milnes, and that if they were living in his house, and not in one of their own, they might be allowed to remain on the island. He was by no means sure that they would not be sent away at once and, when on Sunday, July 4, 1813, a note was delivered at his house to say that they had landed, he was filled with mingled hopes and fears.

> We, of course, felt much agitated," he wrote. "The mingled emotions of joy and hope and fear which were felt cannot easily be described. A companion in labor, whose arrival for seven long years I had been wishing for, having now actually set his foot on earth in this land remote from our native isle, made me very glad. My Mary, who had long wished and prayed for a pious companion to share our solitude, was overjoyed on the arrival of Mrs. Milne. But what would be their reception? Whether they would be allowed to remain, or whether they would be driven away, were all equally uncertain, though not equally probable. That which was not wished for, was greatly to be feared.

Morrison immediately went down to the tavern, about ten minutes' walk away, where Mr. and Mrs. Milne were waiting, praying to God as he did so for blessing and guidance. After they had greeted each other, Mrs. Milne was sent home in a sedan chair while the two men went to see the Portuguese Governor to get permission for them to remain. They were received cordially and no objection was raised at the moment.

Next day Morrison called on the Chinese Governor to report the arrival and get his permission for the

Milnes to stay on the island. The Governor made various objections, but finally said he would do nothing actively against it. He would consider Mr. Milne as a Chinese student. During the next few days, however, Morrison learned that there was growing hostility among the English and Portuguese. The Roman Catholics protested to the Governor, the Senate met and it was decreed in full council "that Mr. Milne should not remain."

What happened then speaks well for Morrison's determination and grit. Instead of immediately giving in, he tried everything he could to get permission for his friends to remain. He was summoned to the Governor's house and when he arrived, got a very cold reception.

"Does the Padre at your house propose to remain here?" the Governor asked.

"Please your Excellency, for the present, if you please," said Morrison very politely.

"It is absolutely impossible," said the Governor. "He must leave in eight days."

"I entreated him," wrote Morrison,

on one knee, not to persist in this order, to extend the term. The Governor said that it was his orders not to allow people to remain; that the senate and the bishop had required him to act, and he must do it. It was contrary to their religion to allow us to remain. 'I have,' he said, 'been appealed to against you, for publishing books in Chinese at Macao, but from motives of friendship, I forebore addressing the Committee about you.' He finally said that he would extend the eight days to eighteen.

Morrison thought of presenting a petition to him. He also drew out a letter to the bishop, but it had no effect. In fact, the Governor's arguments were unanswerable. He had been ordered by his own Court not to permit any Europeans to stay who were not connected with the Companies; the East India Company had requested the Court not to allow Englishmen there, the Senate had addressed him, the bishop required him to send Milne away; Mr. Roberts said he was not connected with the Company, etc., etc. It was obviously all quite reasonable.

Morrison and Milne approached Mr. Roberts, who said that he would not himself mind Milne remaining as Morrison's assistant, if he had the power to do this. Morrison suggested that Milne might be appointed as his assistant for a short time, perhaps till an answer was received from the Court saying whether or not they would print the Dictionary. If they decided not to do that, Milne could go. Or perhaps Mr. Roberts might ask the Portuguese to allow Milne to stay for two seasons till he had learned the language. Mr. Roberts felt he could not promise either of these. If Milne would go away at the end of the season, he would, however, ask the Governor to let him remain until then. Morrison, hoping that the Portuguese might after all agree to let him stay longer, would not agree to this, and Mr. Roberts was not pleased.

It seemed to be a deadlock, but Morrison was not beaten. He arranged to send Milne to his own house at Canton, to wait for the return of the Company's traders, next season. This would give him the chance to learn something of the language under Morrison's two native teachers.

Mrs. Milne, of course, was not allowed to go to Canton, but permission for her to remain in Macao with Mrs. Morrison was granted. For four months Milne remained at Canton and towards the end of this time, on October 14th, a daughter was born to him and Mrs. Milne.

In August Morrison went to Canton to see Milne. He found him busily engaged with his studies but working in a very hot and uncomfortable room, and obviously suffering a great deal from the terrific heat.

What to arrange about him was worrying Morrison considerably. His own position was not as secure as he would have liked. His success as interpreter for the Company had begun to alarm the Chinese authorities, and they were demanding very full information about him. They were sure that no foreigner could have such a command of their language without assistance from native teachers, and as this was strictly forbidden trouble seemed likely to follow. Morrison, realizing this, decided that he had better dismiss his assistants for a time, and he began to consider whether he and Milne had perhaps better leave Canton and Macao and begin a new mission at Java and Malacca.

In September Morrison returned to Canton and remained there for some months. His time was very much filled with his official duties but he was in daily touch with Milne and able to help him considerably in his studies. In January 1814, the two missionaries decided that Milne should make a tour through the chief Chinese settlements in the Malay Archipelago to distribute copies of the New Testament in Chinese that had just been printed. There is an entry in Morrison's diary about this on the last day of 1813.

> I bless the Lord that this year the New Testament has been completed in Chinese and is now nearly all printed. Oh, that it may be the means of great good. Lord, own it as Thine own Word.

Besides distributing copies of the New Testament, two thousand copies of which he took with him, Milne took ten thousand tracts and five thousand copies of a Catechism. It all had to be arranged very secretly for fear the authorities should find out and take action. Already about a hundred copies of St. Luke's Gospel had been burned by the Roman Catholics at Macao, by the Bishop's orders, and the Chinese would certainly be prepared to do the same.

The journey lasted nearly seven months and extended over fourteen hundred miles. There were other objects the missionaries had in view besides the distribution of the Christian books. Milne was to try to find a quiet and peaceful place, where they could fix the chief seat of the Chinese mission they hoped to start, and where there was no persecuting government to harass them. He was to take notes, also, about the Chinese population in the various places he visited, which might help the missionaries to decide the best means for spreading the Gospel throughout the Archipelago. Lastly, Morrison told him to find out what possibility there was of getting printed a volume of dialogues in Chinese and English that he had written, with the idea of assisting other missionaries in learning Chinese.

Milne, writing about his early departure from Canton, says:

> to be so early deprived of the tuition of Mr. Morrison, to whose personal kindness I am no less indebted, than to his attainments in Chinese literature, is very painful to me. It is, however, a great ease to my mind to leave my family under the kind care of Mr. and Mrs. Morrison.

The journey was a difficult one for Milne, especially as he did not yet know much Chinese. At the same time he received a good deal of unexpected kindness from

Sir Stamford Raffles, Lieut-Governor of Java, who helped him in every way he could, giving him letters of introduction to British officers and native princes. At Malacca, also, Colonel Farquhar, the Resident, proved to be a good friend.

During Milne's absence Morrison was working hard at his Chinese Dictionary, encouraged because the Company was not only printing it but was sending out from England a press and a printer for this special purpose. His private affairs at this time were a mixture of worry and happiness. On April 17th, a son was born to him and his wife and two days later a message from Peking arrived, ordering a search to be made throughout Macao for Chinese Christians. Abel Yun, one of Morrison's assistants, was obliged to leave his home and take refuge in one of the European churches.

This further evidence of the determined opposition of the Chinese authorities to Christianity made Morrison more than ever sure that he must find new headquarters. Then, only two months later, something happened that showed the missionary that his patient efforts had not been entirely in vain. Tsae A-Ko, one of his native helpers who had to fly from Canton because of the persecution there, arrived at Macao and asked to be baptized into the Christian faith.

In his journal Morrison wrote full details of this convert. He had come in contact with the missionary when he was twenty-one and he was now twenty-seven.

At first he had not understood much about Christianity, and he was so hot tempered that Morrison had dismissed him from his service. But A-Ko continued to come to morning and evening services on Sundays and by degrees he became convinced that above everything he wished to become a Christian.

Morrison wrote:

> At a spring of water issuing from the foot of a lofty hill by the seaside, away from human observation, I baptized, in the name of the Father, Son and Holy Spirit, the person whose character and profession has been given above. Oh, that the Lord may cleanse him from all sin in the blood of Jesus and purify his heart by the influence of the Holy Spirit. May he be the first fruits of a great harvest; one of the millions who shall believe.

It was the following September when Milne returned to China again, and he and Morrison discussed fully their future plans. From what Milne told him, Morrison was sure that Malacca was the place where a permanent settlement should be made. He would have preferred the mission to have been in China or at least in Canton or Macao, but he knew this was not possible. They discussed the whole project very fully, and the result was that in the following April, Milne and his wife sailed for Malacca to make a permanent settlement there, and Morrison wrote to the directors of the London Missionary Society setting out what he wished to do and why.

He pointed out that in the present state of China, printing was very difficult and it was uncertain that any missionary could long reside there. It was desirable, therefore, to obtain a station under some European Protestant government, near to China, where the chief seat of the Chinese Mission could be fixed.

He suggested that Milne should go to Malacca and obtain ground there where the Mission could be built, and where a Chinese Free School could be started. He suggested beginning a monthly magazine in Chinese and that the Mission Station should be for work among Chinese, Malays and missions on that side of India, and that printing in Chinese, Malay and English should be begun. He said that a missionary journal in English, for missionaries of various denominations, should be considered, and that there ought to be religious services conducted in the Chinese language. He added that as his work on the Chinese Dictionary did not allow him to give his whole time to translation, Milne might undertake to translate some parts of the Old Testament, so that together they might translate the whole Bible.

He had just dispatched this report to London when he received two bequests, the first from William Parry, an official of the East India Company who had died at Canton, for a thousand Spanish dollars; the second from the late Mr. Roberts, the Company's Superintendent at Macao—who had recently died—for the same amount.

He heard also that the Bible Society in London had made a second grant of five hundred pounds towards the cost of printing the Chinese Testaments, with a promise of further grants towards the cost of printing the Old Testament when this work began.

Morrison saw these bequests and contributions as a direct answer to his prayers for the new mission—to be known as the Ultra-Ganges Mission—and the spring of 1815 found him full of the hope that his worst trials might be over and the work he so loved might go on to complete success.

CHAPTER 8

Trials and Triumph

1815-1816

ll through Morrison's career as a missionary it seemed as if hope and disappointment followed close upon one another. At the end of 1814 he and Milne had definitely decided on the establishment of the new mission at Malacca, and they were confident that it would be a success. Before Milne actually left in April, 1815, however, Morrison realized that when this happened he would be left in utter loneliness.

His wife's health had never been good. Now, at the beginning of 1815, Morrison was told that unless she returned for a long visit to England she would certainly die. It was a heavy and bitter blow. His own work was far too important for him to leave China even for a few months, and he knew that he must let her and their two children go alone. There is only one brief entry in his journal about this.

> Jan. 21st. I parted from my dear family. Mrs. Morrison's long-continued ill-health making a return to her native country absolutely necessary.

Milne, writing about it, says rather more.

> In countries where friends of a congenial mind and edifying conversation are but few, it is no easy matter for the members of a Christian family to separate; and especially where urgent and important duties of a local nature prevent those that are in health from accompanying, and rendering the needful attentions to, the afflicted party. But it is a trial which duty often calls upon them to bear. The members of the Chinese Mission have had it to encounter more than once. It was severely felt by them all in the present instance, especially by Mr. and Mrs. Morrison themselves. Yet they considered that his labors were at that time of so important and urgent a nature, as that the suspension of them even for a few months would have been a great loss to the cause in which he was engaged, and hoped that, as they were separating at the call of duty, God would support their minds and afford his gracious protection.

There is no doubt that the departure of his wife and family was a heavy trial to Morrison, but it is characteristic of him that he hardly mentions it and that he bore the separation bravely. As always, his work came first. He went on with his official duties to the East India Company and his work on the Dictionary quietly and steadily, putting his loneliness aside. In the autumn another blow, which might have made it necessary for him to leave China, fell.

When Morrison had dispatched copies of his Chinese New Testament to the London Missionary Society he had asked them not to give a copy to the East India Company, being sure that this would not be wise. Somehow or other, however, a copy reached the librarian of the Company, together with an account of the official transactions of the Missionary Society, containing, of course, a full account of Morrison's missionary work in China.

As Morrison had foreseen, the Directors of the East India Company were thoroughly alarmed. They were afraid that as Morrison was in their employ the Chinese Government might decide to obstruct the trade of the Company, so they passed a vote dismissing him from their service, erased his name from their register and sent an official letter about this to the President of their Committee in Canton. The moment this order was carried out it would mean that his salary of a thousand pounds a year would cease, and the Chinese authorities would certainly order him to leave China.

What actually happened is rather amusing. The chiefs of the East India Company in Canton had not the slightest wish to lose Morrison's services, which they considered extremely valuable. They were obliged to tell him what had happened, but they added that they would not enforce the order at the moment. They wrote:

> We feel it necessary to acquaint you, that the Honorable the Court of Directors, having been informed that you have printed and published in China the New Testament, together with several religious tracts in the Chinese language, and having further understood that the circulation of these translations has been effected in defiance of an edict of the Emperor of China, rendering the publisher of such works liable to capital punishment, are apprehensive that serious mischief may possibly arise to the British Trade in China, and have in consequence directed that your present connection with the Honorable Company should be discontinued.

> Notwithstanding these orders, we are under so strong an impression of the importance of your services, and so well assured, from our personal knowledge and past experience, of your prudence and discretion in forbearing to place yourself in a situation which may be calculated to implicate the national interests, that we have resolved to postpone giving any effect to any part of the above instructions until we receive further orders on the subject.

They went on to say that they were sure that the Company had acted on incorrect information, and asked Morrison to give them such information and explanations on the subject as would enable them to prove this to the Company in England, which, of course, Morrison immediately did.

He pointed out that the Emperor's edict mentioned had been against the Roman Catholics, and that he was sure that his name, except as interpreter and translator to the Company, was unknown to the Chinese Authorities. Therefore there was no "defiance" in his conduct. The books he had translated had been circulated with great caution and in a way that could not easily be traced to him; even if they *were* traced, he would not expect the East India Company to protect him. He ended by saying that his private pursuits were exactly the same as they were at the commencement of his connection with the Company.

This explanation was at once sent to London. What the East India Company would have done about it will never be known, because before a reply could be received a Government Embassy arrived from London on a special mission to the Chinese Emperor at Peking. Morrison, as interpreter, was asked to go with the Embassy. After that, of course, the question of his dismissal from the East India Company was at an end. If the Government considered him a suitable person to employ, then the East India Company could hardly do less!

The reason for this mission was occasioned by the English-American war. Enthusiastically, an English man-of-war had captured an American merchantman and brought her into Macao as a prize. Then they proceeded to chase an American schooner up the Canton River to within ten miles of Canton. Naturally the Chinese

Government were furious at these warlike proceedings in their territorial waters, and the East India Company were forced for a time to leave Canton. The whole position was so serious that the English Government felt a special mission to Peking was absolutely necessary.

It was certainly a great tribute to Morrison's reputation as a Chinese scholar that he should have gone in personal attendance on the Ambassador. It was also a great delight for him to see Peking, which he knew he would never have reached in any other way.

The mission was on the whole a failure, although a local settlement that enabled the East India Company still to trade at Canton was afterwards secured.

The reason for this failure is interesting. When they arrived at Tung-Chow, one day's journey from the capital, Lord Amhurst, the Ambassador, was told that on being presented to the Emperor he would be required to Kotow, which meant that he must kneel down and with hands extended strike the ground three times with his head as a mark of devotion and submission, and this he must do three times. Lord Amhurst, representing the King of England, sturdily refused to do this unless a Chinese official of equal rank did the same in front of a portrait of King George the Third. They argued about it for eight days, and finally the Chinese Duke in charge of the ceremonies pretended to agree. On August 28th the party set out, and after traveling all night reached Peking at break of day.

They were then hurried "unwashed and undressed" as Morrison remarked, "to the door of the palace."

Lord Amhurst protested that, seeing the temperature was 100°F, he was neither physically fit nor suitably dressed to see the Emperor. On this, the Chinese, with concealed satisfaction—they were not at all keen on the Embassy seeing the Emperor—misinformed the Emperor as to the reasons for delay, with the result that he angrily issued a decree ordering the Ambassador to depart at once. On the same day, without any rest, they were taken back to Tung-Chow, again traveling all through the night.

On the return journey the Embassy traveled south by the Grand Canal to Chingkiang, up the Yangtze to the Poyang Lake, and then through Kiangsi and Kwantung direct to Canton. Morrison enjoyed the journey greatly. It gave him a knowledge of Chinese life which his residence on the outskirts of Canton could not give him, and he visited temples and mosques, and the old College of the White Stag where Chu-fu-tze, the great commentator of Confucius, taught seven hundred years ago. Judging from the following extract from his diary, he was not greatly impressed by the Buddhist temple worship.

I am now writing in a temple in which are upwards of a hundred priests, and as many idols. About fifty priests worship images of Buddha, with morning and evening prayers that last forty minutes. There are three images placed in a line; before these the priests burn tapers, offer incense and recite prayers, sometimes kneeling and repeating over and over again the same invocation, sometimes putting the forehead to the ground in token of adoration or supplication. Day after day and year after year this is gone through, but they never bring together the people of every rank and age to instruct them. Indeed they are not qualified, for they are illiterate and uninstructed themselves, the mere performers of ceremonies.

The journey to Peking and back with its change of scene and exercise was of great benefit to Morrison's health. He returned to Canton with renewed energy, and the news that Milne had baptized his first convert at Malacca gave him great joy. But he was very lonely without his friend or his family. In one letter he wrote:

This is a very tiresome place; lonely and in continual apprehension. I hope the Almighty Arm which has been my defense hitherto will still preserve me from evil.

In another letter he says:

I am still engaged in translation and in compiling the Dictionary, which is very laborious work. My courage and perseverance almost fail me. This is a very lonely situation. I am under continual dread of the arm of the oppressor, and more than that, the natives who assist me are hunted from place to place and sometimes seized.

To add to his worries, news from home about his family was infrequent. Once the ships of the season arrived, but with no news. He wrote home:

I am now likely to be kept in uncertainty and suspense until September. I cannot assist those who have the first claim on my utmost regard, but there is a Providence. I have become much of a recluse. I very rarely go to the Company or anywhere else to dine. I have the same dish week after week—Irish stew and dried roots, which I eat with Chinese chopsticks. I am well as usual and writing from seven in the morning till nine or ten at night.

CHAPTER 9

Joy and Sorrow

1817-1822

he Dictionary was not printed without difficulty. The Chinese printers had to be dismissed for fear of persecution, and, with great difficulty, Portuguese were engaged. Some of the blocks from which the book was printed had been seized by the Viceroy, and others were hidden in a corner of the printing office to prevent this. Some of these were also destroyed, this time by white ants, who made a pleasant meal of them.

In spite of all this, however, the work steadily continued. Early in 1817 the first printed copies of Volume I were issued and in the same year the University of Glasgow conferred on Morrison the honorary degree of Doctor of Divinity, in recognition of his work. His work was also recognized by many of the leading Universities in Europe and America and he had many letters from leading scholars.

There is no doubt that Morrison's powers of work were enormous and extraordinary. In 1819 he completed the tremendous task of translating the Old and New Testaments. In just over twelve years, in spite of all the hindrances he had from the Chinese he had, with very little help, mastered one of the most difficult forms of human speech and writing, completed the translation, published his Chinese Grammar and many smaller works, besides making good progress with the Dictionary. Even if he had been able to give his whole time to study and work, this output would have been extraordinary. To accomplish it in the way he did shows that his gift for languages and his powers of concentration were extremely unusual.

One very interesting point in his character was his breadth of mind in religious matters. He took what he considered best from all denominations of the Christian Churches and translated them. On the tenth anniversary of his landing in China, he wrote:

The Church of Scotland supplied me with a Catechism—the Congregational Churches afforded us a form for a Christian assembly—and the Church of England has supplied us with a Manual of Devotion as a help to those who are not sufficiently instructed to conduct social worship without such aid. (This refers to his translation of part of the Book of Common Prayer). We are of no party. We recognize but two divisions of our fellow-creatures—the righteous and the wicked—those who fear God and those who do not. Grace be with all them that love our Lord Jesus Christ in sincerity.

On November 11, 1818, the foundation stone of the College at Malacca planned by Morrison and Milne was laid. It was a plain building, with a deep veranda back and front and extending at both ends. On each side were arranged the Chinese and English printing offices, the schools and apartments for the Chinese masters, etc. It faced the sea and was shaded by a row of senna trees. From the very first the College was a success.

In the same year the Principal of the University of Edinburgh asked Morrison to furnish him with details as to the number of poor, sick, orphans and lunatics, etc., in China, how they were cared for and whether by imperial or local taxes. He wanted these facts because he was collecting materials for a history of the poor over the globe. He could not have had the slightest idea of the difficulties involved in giving him this information, but Morrison, thorough as usual, endeavored to do so.

He got in touch with Dr. Livingstone who, it will be remembered, had been his wife's doctor, and the doctor wrote a paper on the subject which was published in the Indo-Chinese Gleaner, a quarterly magazine started by

Morrison and Milne. This led Dr. Livingstone on to the study of Chinese medicine, and to the purchase through Morrison of a Chinese medical library of more than eight hundred volumes.

Morrison was also very interested, and he began to study the herbs used by the Chinese in the healing of diseases, finally opening a small dispensary of his own where the poor could get proper medical treatment for a small cost. For two hours each day, overworked though he was, he worked in the dispensary, employing a Chinese doctor to help him in dealing with the crowds who came for help. Dr. Livingstone gave what help he could, and for some time the little dispensary continued in its healing work. It was not labor in vain. The experiment was reported to the Missionary Society and twenty years later they sent out their first medical missionary, Dr. William Lockhart. There is no doubt that Morrison was a true pioneer.

In February 1819, Mrs. Milne died. Both she and Milne had for some years had bad health caused by the hard work they had undertaken. In 1817 they stayed for some time at Macao with considerable benefit to both of them. Mrs. Milne, however, was sure that as far as she was concerned the improvement could not last, and she was right. She had lost one baby son in 1816, and her little daughter Sarah died in 1817. Her husband wrote that "she never afterwards recovered her natural vivacity."

Another son was born in February 1819, but fever and dysentery followed and in March she died. She left four small children for her broken-hearted husband to look after, but both he and Morrison knew that it was unlikely that Milne himself would live many more years. His lungs were already badly affected. The life of a missionary in the Far East in those days was a precarious one and that of a missionary's wife even more so.

Morrison knew this, and his joy at welcoming his own family back from England in August, 1820, must have been mixed with anxiety for fear his wife's health would once more break down. They had been separated for nearly six years, and after a few weeks together in Macao he was obliged once more to take up his duties in Canton and leave his family behind at Macao.

He was away from them until the summer of 1821 when, at the end of the trading season, he rejoined them. Their house was by the sea, and he and his wife with their two children used to walk happily along the shore almost every evening. It seemed as if now, at last, Morrison's loneliness was over. But the worst trial of all was near. In June, Mary Morrison was suddenly attacked by cholera and two days later she died in her husband's arms. She was buried in a plot of land purchased by the East India Company to become the Protestant burial ground in Macao.

His children clung to him in their sorrow. His little daughter Rebecca, now nine years old, asked him anxiously if he must go back to Canton, where she knew that she, as a girl, could not go. He had to say he must. Happily Dr. and Mrs. Livingstone came to the rescue and promised to look after her during the winter months. John, who was seven, went with Morrison to Canton. Early the following year, however, Morrison decided that as it was impossible for him to look after his children himself, he must send them back to England. Rebecca went with Mr. and Mrs. Maloney in the Company's ship *Kent*, and John in the *Atlas* under the surgeon's care.

This was in March. The only person left on that side of the globe whom Morrison really loved was Milne, who had been obliged to leave his work and go to Singapore in the hopes that the voyage and rest might restore him to health. He wrote to his friend on March 23rd from Singapore and his letter brought alarm and the presentiment of further sorrow to Morrison.

"I am still here," wrote Milne, "though I do not feel myself improved much."

Morrison's reply shows his deep anxiety.

I have received your letter and deeply regret the afflicting news which it contains. O that God may spare your life and restore your health! I am going on mourning all the day, and unprofitable servant. Alas! I write this fearing you are already beyond the reach of letters. Farewell! God bless the children.

What he feared had already happened. On June 2, 1822, Milne had died. It was a very bitter grief to Morrison. He and Milne were more than colleagues; they were close friends. They wrote to each other as Robert and William, and Milne's death now left Morrison entirely alone, without anyone to whom he could confide his worries or with whom he could discuss his problems. It meant, too, that he was obliged to postpone his own long deferred visit to England. It was necessary, he felt, that he should visit Malacca to try to arrange for someone to "carry on the Chinese department."

Writing home to a friend he said:

To the death of my beloved Mary that of Milne is now added. Dear William died on June 2, 1822. I do not repine at the dispensations of Providence, but I have wept much on being left alone and desolate...I have been fifteen years in this country and one-half of these years quite alone, but God has borne with my infirmities and has blessed the labor of my hands. My present health is still wonderfully good. I did not at first suppose I should have lived as long as I have. I hope I, too, shall die at my post.

To his sister-in-law, two days later, he wrote:

I have felt and still feel very much cast down. I am so friendless in one sense. My parents have long been dead—all of you are far from me. Those I loved have been taken away. The heathen around me are inhospitable and void of affection for strangers.

Yet, oh how much have I to be thankful for. God save me from being ungrateful to Him. He has given me a hope to trust His grace and to be interested in His salvation, and He has brought me to honor in His Church and He has given me abundant provision for all my bodily comforts...I enclose £300 for the benefit of my dear children. I wish to adopt little Robert Milne as my son and support him with my own (John) Robert. This must be arranged with the executors.

It was a brave letter and showed, in the midst of his loneliness, his love and consideration for others. To Morrison it must have seemed that the rest of his life would be lonely. He did not know that two years later happiness was to return to him, a happiness that was to endure until nearly the end of his life.

CHAPTER 10

Fire and Furlough

1822-1825

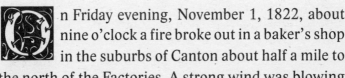n Friday evening, November 1, 1822, about nine o'clock a fire broke out in a baker's shop in the suburbs of Canton about half a mile to the north of the Factories. A strong wind was blowing and the fire spread rapidly among the crowded wooden houses. Fire engines belonging to the Company and the Chinese merchants were called out, but the water supply was so poor and the streets so crowded and narrow that they were not much use. The Chinese, mad with fear, did nothing to help. All they thought about was rescuing as many of their own possessions as they could. The panic was dreadful and made worse by armed bandits seizing the opportunity for plunder.

Finding that their efforts to stop the fire were in vain, members of the Company kept an anxious watch all night from the terrace of the English Chief's house, and shortly after midnight orders were sent to the fleet ordering boats and men from each ship to come up river and be ready to help.

Just before daybreak on Saturday, Morrison wrote three appeals in Chinese, begging on behalf of all the Factories that the authorities would order houses in front of the fire to be pulled down in order to stop it spreading further.

One of these letters was given to a Chinese Official standing watching the fire, who merely "looked frigidly displeased at its contents"; another was given to an Official who refused to take it or read it. The third was taken by Morrison himself addressed to the Governor. The men in charge of the city gate would not allow him to pass, and the letter was given to an officer who disappeared with it.

The Governor sent back the letter unopened because it was sealed with the private seal of one of the members of the Company and not with the Company's official seal. It was returned to him with the explanation that the Company's seal had been removed to a place of safety and was not accessible. Later on he said he had not read it. The fire, he said, was "Heaven's will." Instead of trying to stop it, he spent the night on the city walls engaged in prayer to heaven for deliverance. "Next day," said Morrison, "he came to view the ruins and wept over them!"

By eight o'clock on Saturday morning the fire had reached the Factories. The foreigners were driven to the river's edge by the fire and smoke, while houses crashed behind them. The flames spread across China Street, through the Hong merchants' Factories, and devoured most of the European Factories. Then the wind changed, and the fire swept westwards across the suburbs and along the edge of the river for about a mile and a half until there was nothing more left to burn. Thousands of shops and houses and scores of people were destroyed. At one spot Morrison records that twenty-seven people were trampled to death in a scramble for dollars when a robber cut open a bag that a man was carrying on his back.

By Sunday morning there was a mass of smoking ruins where the Factories had stood. Some of the walls were still standing but looked ready to fall at any moment. The Chinese refused to pull them down, and this had to be done by the officers and men of the fleet, while the Company's officials were busy overseeing the removal of the company's funds, about seven hundred thousand dollars, to a place of safety, and driving off robbers who were busy looking for loot among the ruins.

"This fire," wrote Morrison, "was not exceeded by the fire of London of 1666." The London fire had burned an area of about a mile and a half wide; the

Canton fire was larger than that and a larger number of people were made homeless.

Morrison comments also that the Chinese officials and merchants showed themselves entirely selfish in their attitude towards the Europeans. Not one of them volunteered a night's lodging, or a single meal to the houseless and fasting "foreign devils." He adds, "From this censure the Chinese servants must be exempted. They generally stuck to their masters and aided honestly in saving their property." Among the things of Morrison's that were destroyed was a hundred pounds' worth of paper that he had been intending to send to Malacca for a new edition of the New Testament.

Six months' leave was due to him, so in January, two months after the fire, he sailed on the *Duchess of Argyle* for Malacca. His leave certainly afforded him relief from the Company's work and a very welcome change, but it could hardly be called a holiday, because he spent most of it in hard work, visiting Singapore two or three times to discuss with Sir Stamford Raffles, the Resident there, the possibility of starting an Anglo-Chinese College like the one at Malacca, and reorganizing the Malacca college so that Milne's work there could be carried on.

He could not stay as long in Malacca as he would have liked, owing to an urgent recall from the East India Company. Trouble had arisen some time before between the traders and the Chinese, and Morrison was needed to help settle it. It took a long time before both parties managed to find an agreement that would enable trade to be started again without either side too obviously sacrificing its dignity—the dispute had begun with an assault by some Chinese on a party of English sailors and had led to casualties on both sides. Morrison had escaped the beginning of the affair by being in Malacca, but he had a wearisome time helping to settle it when he returned to Canton.

One great joy during this time was the return of one of his old teachers, Leang A-Fa, with his wife and small son. A-Fa's wife had also become a Christian and now both parents wanted the child to be baptized. "Oh, that this small Chinese family," wrote Morrison, "may be made the means of spreading the truth around them in this pagan land."

Leang A-Fa had suffered for his faith. For printing a tract he had been put into prison and beaten with bamboo rods, and yet for eight years he had steadfastly remained a Christian. Morrison, knowing that before long he would be able to go back to England for his long overdue furlough, ordained Leang A-Fa to the office of evangelist, so that he could be left in charge during his master's absence.

Satisfied that Christian work would be carried on while he was away, Morrison left Canton on December 5, 1823, sailing in the *Waterloo*, taking with him his Chinese library of several thousand volumes. Shortly before he sailed he reported with joy to Sir George Staunton, "the Dictionary is all printed!"

The voyage lasted a hundred days. They called at Cape Town where he met the famous Robert Moffat, and at St. Helena, where he visited Napoleon's tomb, cutting a slip from the willow which hung over the grave and planting it on board. The voyage ended at Salcombe in Devon, where he "disembarked in a smuggler" and set off at once by road for London.

In London he was presented to King George IV, who graciously accepted a copy of the Bible in Chinese, with a map of Peking. What Morrison probably appreciated more was that he was elected a Fellow of the Royal Society. He was also invited to a dinner given by the Honorable Directors of the East India Company, who now wanted to honor the man whose name they had struck from their register a few short years before. The Directors of the London Missionary Society also gave him a great welcome when he formally handed over to them a copy of his newly completed Chinese Bible and the Anglo-Chinese Dictionary. It must all have been very gratifying to Morrison.

He wanted to go north to visit his family as soon as possible. He was delayed, however, by difficulties with the Customs. They refused to allow him to take his valuable Chinese library away until a large sum in duty had been paid. As he had spent more than £2,000 in purchasing it with the idea of presenting it to the nation, he was considerably annoyed.

Sir George Staunton applied to the Treasury to allow the books to pass free, and endless delays followed. It was not until the Chancellor of the Exchequer, Sir Robert Peel, and other celebrities had been interviewed, that the books were finally released. The Customs Authorities were extremely reluctant to lose an opportunity to charge duty.

Morrison had not intended to stay long in England, but the leading Missionary Societies all wanted his presence at meetings up and down the country. For months he went from one end of England and Scotland to the other, visiting his own people in Newcastle, his children in Lancashire, Milne's orphans in Scotland, Orientalists in Paris, speaking and preaching in many of the principal towns in England and in Ireland.

His friends were so anxious to see him that they were inconsiderate. He wrote:

> I am laboring from morning to night and from day to day for my kindred and for my children and for the public, and sacrificing all personal considerations, and still I do not give satisfaction. My friends are most unmerciful, requiring of me more than I can do and seemingly offended because I do not perform the impossible.

In actual fact he very nearly did. His time was occupied from morning to night and not often on his own concerns. It is pleasant to record, however, that when visiting his children in Liverpool he met Miss Elizabeth Armstrong and did manage to find sufficient time to find out that he loved her and wanted to make her his wife. In November they were married and settled down together in Hackney with his two children. Here he continued his literary work, undisturbed by the amusements of the children or the arrival of constant visitors.

CHAPTER 11

China Again

1826-1833

t was in February 1826, that, with his wife and family, he sailed once more for China to take up his missionary duties again and to resume his position with the East India Company. He had been informed by them that this time his appointment was only for three years, but in actual fact it continued until the cessation of the Company's Charter, and on his death a pension was granted to his family as a testimony to his merits and services.

During his time in England he had managed to form a School of Oriental Languages that he hoped would be of great use to intending missionaries. He had given suggestions to the various Missionary Societies for overcoming ignorance and apathy about China at home, and had seen working parties formed in various parts of the country to aid the College at Malacca. His time there had certainly given a stimulus to the interest in the mission so dear to his heart.

The voyage was an adventurous one. Gales, danger of fire, and a mutiny, enlivened the journey. At Macao, which they reached in September, he found that during his two years' absence his house and furniture had been so neglected that they were almost destroyed and, worse still, his library had been almost all eaten by white ants. He managed to make arrangements for the comfort of his family while his house was being rebuilt; then he went on to Canton, to take up again his lonely life there. There was plenty of work for him to do for the Company, but he had to decide what his other work must now be. He had translated the Bible and his Dictionary was finished and published.

"If I go on learning the polite language of China," he wrote, "I may go on learning to my dying hour, but I can write intelligibly in Chinese; therefore I think I had better desist from learning pagan law and teach Christianity in the simple Chinese phrase."

He finally decided to begin notes on the Holy Scriptures in Chinese, also a work called *Domestic Instructions*, derived from Divine Revelation. Two more projects were the preparation of a system of references for the Bible, with chronological, historical, and literary notes, and a Dictionary of the Canton dialect. He opened a language school for anyone in the Factories who wanted to learn Chinese. He helped informing a local museum called "The British Museum in China," and opened a coffee shop for the sailors of the East India Fleet, in whom he had always been very interested.

His work with the East India Company was by no means always pleasant. There had been changes among the chief officers of the Company, and some of the men who were now over him attempted to interfere with his work and lord it over him in a manner he deeply resented. At one time the situation was so intolerable that he very nearly resigned his post. His own health and strength were beginning to fail and he felt it was all too much for him. Before the letter of resignation he wrote was delivered, however, changes among the chief officials of the Company made him reconsider such a drastic step.

Among his official duties he found time to visit sick and dying sailors and to give what assistance he could to any Chinese he knew was in distress. One instance of this can be given.

A small French ship with wine, silk and treasure put into port in Cochin China for repairs. The vessel was so badly damaged that she was condemned, and a Chinese junk was chartered to take the cargo and passengers to Macao. Just before they reached Macao the Chinese crew massacred all the passengers except two who leapt into the sea. One of these drowned, but the other was picked up by a fishing boat and brought to Macao. The junk was traced, the captain and crew taken prisoners, tortured and condemned to death, being brought to Macao to confront the one survivor before they were executed.

One of the condemned men had taken no part in the massacre and had done his best to warn the Europeans. The survivor, Francisco Mangiapan, knew this and wanted him to be set free. Morrison gladly gave his services as interpreter, with the result that the man was finally acquitted. And for once Morrison's name was applauded by the Chinese in Canton, so that for a short time he was the hero of the hour. He took it, as he had taken their dislike, calmly and quietly. Neither applause nor hatred made very much difference to him. They certainly did not prevent him from continuing his work, however difficult it might be. He took whatever came, in his stride and still carried on. Once in Macao his library was seriously damaged by a fire that broke out next door. All his books were injured and some completely destroyed. All he said about it was: "M—— said it was a judgment on me for being so fond of the gay bindings!" He seemed, as he grew older, to be developing a sense of humor. Certainly, he had mellowed very considerably in the last few years.

So things went on as the years passed, in hard and tiring work, and for six months of the year and sometimes longer, without the comfort of his wife and family. The separation necessary because of the restrictions of Canton was a great trial to Morrison, and this became more acute as time went on and both his health and his wife's began to suffer. There were now six children in the family, two by the first marriage and four by the second, and Morrison loved his wife and children and wanted to be with them.

His eldest son, John Robert, went with his father to Canton when he was sixteen to continue his Chinese studies there. This was in 1830, and in September of that year the boy was appointed Chinese Translator to the British merchants in Canton. Towards the end of 1832 he went with an expedition to Siam and Cochin China. It was a trading expedition. In a letter to his daughter Rebecca, Morrison wrote: "I have advised his being a merchant, with a constant reference to his being a merchant missionary. I trust he will not be less zealous nor useful because he is an unpaid lay missionary."

Morrison missed his son so much, that he took his second son, then only seven years old, to be with him in Canton. It was an anxious time for him. His wife's health was growing worse, and he was desperately afraid that she would have to return to England. He was worried, too, about his official position. It seemed very probable that the East India Company's Charter would soon expire and when this happened his official appointment would also end. What was worse, although he had now served the Company for twenty-five years, they had refused to give him a pension when he retired. He was now over fifty and, as he had never taken the least care of himself, but had worked unremittingly, he was, in his own words, "an old man." Many men would have thought it time to retire from the fray and take a well-earned rest. Not so Morrison.

By 1833 he had faced the fact that his wife and family must return home, even though this would be expensive, and he knew that almost any time now his main income might cease. Mrs. Morrison was very reluctant to go. She had noticed how her husband's strength was failing and she hated the thought of leaving him. As the summer went on she was alarmed at his loss of appetite, accompanied by pain on his right side, but the doctor in Macao assured her that it was not serious. She finally consented to sail and passages were booked in the *Inglis*, which was to sail early to December.

John Robert was able to take his father's place temporarily at Canton, and Morrison determined to remain at Macao with his wife and other children until their departure. Knowing that their parting might be the last, every moment with his loved ones was precious. But a month before they were due to sail he was urgently summoned to Canton to translate papers about a fight on an opium ship, where a Chinese and an English sailor had been killed. He was obliged to go.

It was a great trial, and his letters to his wife showed what he felt.

> The most grievous part of the arrangement is the indefinite period of separation," he wrote. "Perhaps you will find kind and faithful friends with whom you would consent to leave the children and return to me. Perhaps the result will prove better than our fears.

A few days later he wrote:

> I am longing for later news than Tuesday last. Macao and Canton are a long way apart—what will England and China be? I almost relent. Feeling would say 'don't go.' But our resolution has been formed—we cannot draw back—who can tell what is in the future? It may be all for the best. 'Thy will be done. O God, we are thine, forsake us not.'

Heart-rending words from a man of such determination. All his life he had been lonely. Now, when at last he had found someone to be a real helpmate to him, someone who loved him and in whom he could confide, he must lose her again. It seemed as if he would be obliged to remain at Canton until his family had sailed, the Company's affairs were dragging along so slowly. He managed, however, to persuade the Committee to allow his son to take his place again, so that the last fortnight might be spent with his family.

Morrison might seem stern and even morose to some people, but his family did not find him so. Here is what his wife said about his returns from Canton to Macao.

His arrival was always hailed with the liveliest demonstrations of delight—even by Caesar who, not satisfied with baying his deep-mouthed welcome at the gate, would endeavor to share with the children in the caresses of his beloved master. The day after these periodical returns from Canton was at all times marked by unusual hilarity and excitement. Books and traps were to be unpacked and replaced—presents distributed—toys examined and arranged; while the dispenser of so much pleasure, largely participating in the gratification he communicated, might be seen with his youngest child in his arms, a second holding his hand, and the rest following him about the house, as he gave the necessary orders for the disposal of the multifarious packages, etc.

A glimpse of the family life on Sundays comes from another of Mrs. Morrison's letters.

Although his manner on the Lord's Day was marked by a more than usual degree of seriousness, which would repress any approach to levity, still there was not in it the slightest tincture of austerity. On these occasions, his usual resort was a retired terrace in the front of his residence, beyond which lay the Bay of Macao, encircled by barren hills—the terrace was shaded by beautifully flowering shrubs and bordered with European plants and flowers. Here, generally accompanied by the whole of his family, the little ones on his knees, or sitting on mats spread on the grass, with their attendants of various nations, Chinese, Portuguese and Caffres, and a favorite Newfoundland dog invariably making one of the group—might be seen the beloved subject of this narrative, whose presence diffused general happiness throughout that favored circle. Often he would express the pleasure this scene afforded him and his grateful sense of the mercies and blessings he enjoyed. Such simple pleasures as those by which he was surrounded, Dr. Morrison enjoyed in a high degree; yet his taste for them was never gratified at the expense of more serious duties.

CHAPTER 12

The Long Day Ends

1833-1834

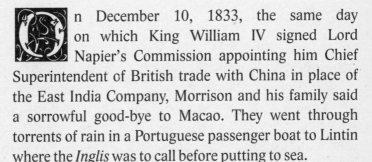n December 10, 1833, the same day on which King William IV signed Lord Napier's Commission appointing him Chief Superintendent of British trade with China in place of the East India Company, Morrison and his family said a sorrowful good-bye to Macao. They went through torrents of rain in a Portuguese passenger boat to Lintin where the *Inglis* was to call before putting to sea.

For that night one of Jardine Matteson's ships stationed there was put at their disposal. Here they waited, most of them helplessly sick because of the rough weather, until December 13th, when the *Inglis* came in sight and some of the officers came to take the passengers on board.

The weather was still very stormy and boarding the ship in the open sea was dangerous. Morrison was persuaded not to go on board, especially as it was already dusk. The next morning the *Inglis* set off on her four months' voyage home, but not before Morrison had sent his wife two short notes.

In one of these he wrote:

> When I consented to part with you I supposed the ship would get under weigh immediately. It has not been so, and if I could have foreseen it, I would have accompanied you and our beloved children to the ship.

In another letter written next day to his wife, he said: "Yesterday morning, at daylight, I watched the *Inglis* conveying you out of sight, with many tears, and much prayer to God for you, my beloved wife, and our dear, dear children."

Morrison thought it more sensible not to renew the lease of his house in Macao, seeing he did not know what would happen to him now the Company's charter had ceased. He sent his son to remove the furniture and surrender the house. Nothing now was left of his happy family life in Macao.

His life's work was drawing very near its close. He was lonely, ill and very worried, but he never thought of deserting his post.

"I am hoping for a more settled state of mind," he wrote to his wife, "after the news from England arrives and the anxiety of the removal is over."

He wrote to her almost every day to within three days of his death, and in these letters it is clear that he knew that his life's work was nearly ended.

It is a matter of joy that God has raised up active laborers in this mission. I do not feel myself now of much importance here to the cause. It will go on without me.

But in another letter he was not so sure about this.

Our friends in England seem to have given up the Chinese Mission—in China. When revolving in my mind which course to pursue, I am hindered by the recollection that of late no measures seem even to have been thought of as to how the mission in China is to be continued, in the event of my removal. I do feel a little desolate, but I hope the Lord will not forsake me.

Two months later he wrote:

I am depressed by finding myself unequal to the literary labors which I attempt. Being quite alone, I am very desirous of more Chinese labor, but my head and my strength fail me. Well, I must be resigned. I have labored abundantly in past days, and have, perhaps, performed my task—all that was allotted me. God forgive me wherein I have erred and sinned.

On January 31, 1834, the last of the Company's ships left Canton, and Morrison went to Macao to await events.

He managed to take an old broken-down house next to his old home, in which to live. Looking at the place where he had been so happy must have hurt him greatly.

> I took a walk out this evening towards the Bishop's Walk, but only got as far as Paiva's Hill," he wrote to his wife. "The whole of the path where you and the children used to go excited such melancholy feelings that although the sun seemed to smile, I could not repress my sadness.

By the middle of the year news arrived that Lord Napier had been appointed to proceed to China to arrange with the Government for the continuation of British trade. Morrison did not know that before Lord Napier left England it had been decided that the post of interpreter to the Government should be offered to him. If he had known, it would not have comforted him much. He was too ill and too lonely.

"Oh how I long to hear of the state of your health," he wrote to his wife. "Tomorrow is the 160th day since you left me. No news from England for nearly seven months. The heat is great, and rarely getting sound sleep, I always feel weary...

"The sight of the children's chairs makes me feel very sad. My beloved children! Oh, when shall I again hear your prayers and kiss your cheeks?"

On July 16th Lord and Lady Napier landed at Macao. Morrison went down to the Chinese customhouse to meet him, and was greeted with obvious delight by him. A meeting of the Factory was summoned to hear the King's Commission read. Here is Morrison's account as he wrote it to his wife.

That which concerned me and you, and our beloved children, I will tell first—I am to be styled 'Chinese Secretary and Interpreter' ănd to have £1,300 a year. I am to wear a vice-consul's coat, with king's buttons, when I can get one! The Government will pay one hundred dollars per month to the College, instead of the Company. His Lordship asked whether I accepted the appointment or not. I told him at once that I did. He said he would forthwith make out my commission.

Pray for me that I may be faithful to my blessed Savior in the new place I have to occupy."

In a few days the Governor went to Canton to complete trading arrangements and Morrison had to accompany him. Two days later he began his last journey. The heat was terrific, and when he had left the frigate in which he had traveled, he was kept all night in an open boat exposed to the moist tropical heat and a storm of rain. When he finally reached his apartments in Canton he was in a state of collapse, and his son John, shocked at his condition, tried to help him in his work as much as he could. The work of translating the negotiations was very long and exacting. Morrison kept going but it was a terrible effort.

On July 25th, he wrote: "Today I have been very low. I thought I must give up the king's service from entire inability to bear the fatigue of it in Canton. God help me, my dear love, I will do nothing rashly. But in walking through the hot sun today from this house of the Company's where Lord Napier is, I was like to drop in the streets, and have been groaning on my couch ever since— being now past eight in the evening. Oh, that I may have cheering accounts from you soon. Good night, my beloved wife. Oh, my beloved children! God be with you all."

On the next day he felt stronger. He was busy the whole day translating a letter from Lord Napier to the Governor of Canton and attending a council board. Then he had to interpret between Lord Napier and one of the Chinese merchants. He felt too ill to walk and went to the house in a sedan chair, closely shut up so that the Chinese might not see him.

The next day was Sunday—his last Sunday on earth. He conducted worship in Chinese, with about a dozen people present. The entry in the journal he kept for his wife written that night closed as follows:

"My name was published yesterday, with the other officers of the king's commission. It stands above the surgeons and chaplains and private secretary."

Next day, July 28th, at eight o'clock in the evening he wrote his last entry:

We have spent another tiresome day, my love, with political squabbles, and got no nearer agreement yet. My health is much the same.

The following day he was dangerously ill with fever and other complications. On Wednesday the assistant surgeon was called in but could give him no relief. The fever continued and although from time to time he rallied, and his son, watching by him, thought he would recover, his body was too worn out for any improvement to last. On Friday evening the fever left him, and he fell into a quiet sleep from which he never awakened.

There is no doubt that his life was shortened by his unsparing devotion to duty. He was only fifty-two when he died, but he had been unfit for work for a long time and only his determination and courage had allowed him to endure so long.

All honors were given to him in his burial. Lord Napier, with all the European and American residents in Canton followed his coffin to the sea, where it was placed on a boat and with John Robert Morrison and the Superintendent of the English Factory in attendance, was taken to Macao for burial. There, where he had worked, suffered, and been happy, he was laid to rest in the cemetery the Company had bought for the burial of his first wife.

Robert Morrison was dead, but his work lived on. His Chinese Dictionary has been superseded, and his translations of the Scriptures have been revised, but no other missionary in China had to work as the only representative of the Protestant missionary force, and no one coming after him had to begin his work without some help in learning the language or without the Bible in the Chinese tongue, and this is entirely because of Morrison's work.

He went out to China as a young man of twenty-five, untested and unknown, with only a fragmentary knowledge of the Chinese language, and with no knowledge of the people among whom he hoped to work. To help him in this work he took the post offered him with the East India Company, knowing that many people would say that he did this for profit and would blame him. This he disregarded, because he knew that only by this means could he be assured of staying in China, and that the money he earned would repay the Missionary Society for what they were spending on his maintenance.

All through his life it was the same. His work for Christ was what mattered to him, not the praise or blame his friends and enemies might give him. He worked alone and unceasingly and when, twenty-five years after he landed at Canton, he reviewed his work, he was able to record a marvelous achievement.

"There is now in Canton a state of society in respect of Chinese, totally different from what I found in 1807," he wrote. "Chinese scholars, missionary students, English presses and Chinese Scriptures, with the public worship of God, have all grown up since that period. I have served my generation and must—the Lord knows when—fall asleep. I feel old age creeping upon me.

Missionary voyages have been performed and the Chinese sought out at various places under European control in the Archipelago, as well as in Siam, at the Loochoo Islands, at Korea, and along the coast of China itself, up to the very walls of Peking. Some tracts written by Protestant missionaries have reached and been read by the Emperor himself.

And all that was directly owing to his work. Steadfastly and alone he had gone on his destined path, never for one moment deflected from it by difficulties, bereavement or the contempt of his enemies. He was wise and humble, always just, always compassionate. He loved his family with a great love, but he never faltered in the path of duty even though this meant separation from them. His determination in the face of appalling difficulties enabled him to do work, which to most men would have seemed impossible. And always, through trials and honors alike, his first thought was to give to the vast pagan world of China the religion of Christ, Whom he served. Truly to all Christians he is a great example.

Like St. Paul he could have said: "According to the grace of God which is given unto me, as a wise master builder, I have laid the foundation, and another buildeth thereon.

"I have learned, in whatsoever state I am, therewith to be content. *I can do all things through Christ which strengtheneth me.*"

Lessons from Morrison's life:

YOUR OBSERVATIONS

_____

_____

_____

_____

_____

_____

_____

_____

_____

_____

_____

_____

_____

_____

_____

_____

_____

_____

_____

_____

_____

_____

_____

_____

_____

_____

_____

_____

_____

_____

_____

_____

_____

_____

DAVID LIVINGSTONE
Missionary to Africa

Facing jealousy from other missionaries, the death of his wife, troubles, delays, worries, hunger, thirst, illness, and the fear of death from the slave-dealers and wild animals, Livingstone was still close to God. His Bible was his solace and he felt the companionship of Jesus Christ even when he was most alone.

Livingstone believed that God had called him to open Africa; and having done so, he left it to others, under God's guidance, to pick up the task where he had finished. Because of the work of David Livingstone, there are thousands of missionaries on the field today; missionaries who love the same Lord Jesus who made Livingstone the hero that he was.

ISBN 1-932307-24-9, $5.99/£4.99 (ages 8-13)

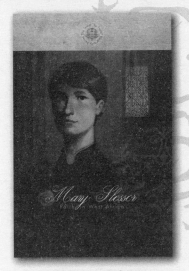

MARY SLESSOR
Faith in West Africa

Perhaps the greatest thing that can be said of Mary Slessor is that she was a born missionary. From her earliest days, her dream was to be a missionary and Calabar (Nigeria) was her mission field. The death of David Livingstone was the catalyst for her missionary call, and in 1876, she went to the African mission field.

"Anywhere, provided it be forward," was one of her most famous sayings and summed up her life. She toiled for forty years in the heart of Nigeria, constantly seeking new tribes and new people to reach with the gospel of Christ. She rescued hundreds of orphans from certain death, prevented wars between tribes, helped to heal the sick, and spoke ceaselessly of the great love of God in sending Jesus Christ.

ISBN 1-932307-25-7, $6.99/£5.99 (ages 14-19)

JOHN WYCLIFFE
Man of Courage

John Wycliffe, the Morning Star of the Reformation, gave us the first English translation of the Bible. A noted scholar and teacher at Oxford, his reliance on the Bible as the sole source of truth stood in stark contrast to the teachings of the Catholic church. His followers went out, teaching and preaching to the common man throughout England.

Bowing himself to the authority of the Bible, his great aim was to bring men to the Word. He saw it as the one great authority, the Law that exceeded all other laws. His life's work continued through men like John Hus and laid the groundwork for Martin Luther, John Calvin, John Knox and the other great men of the Reformation.

ISBN 1-932307-27-3, $5.99/£4.99 (ages 14-19)